UNDERSTANDING PSYCHOLOGY

Understanding Family and Personal Relationships

Christine Wilcox

ReferencePoint Press®

San Diego, CA

ReferencePoint Press®

Printed in the United States

For more information, contact:
ReferencePoint Press, Inc.
PO Box 27779
San Diego, CA 92198
www.ReferencePointPress.com

LIBRARY OF CONGRESS CATALOGING-IN-PUBLICATION DATA

Name: Wilcox, Christine, author.
Title: Understanding Family and Personal Relationships/by Christine Wilcox.
Description: San Diego, CA: ReferencePoint Press, [2017] | Series: Understanding Psychology | Audience: Grade 9 to 12. | Includes bibliographical references and index.
Identifiers: LCCN 2017007636 (print) | LCCN 2017021175 (ebook) | ISBN 9781682822746 (eBook) | ISBN 9781682822739 (hardback)
Subjects: LCSH: Families—Psychological aspects—Juvenile literature. | Interpersonal relations—Juvenile literature. | Love—Juvenile literature.
Classification: LCC HQ519 (ebook) | LCC HQ519 .W545 2017 (print) | DDC 302--dc23
LC record available at https://lccn.loc.gov/2017007636

CONTENTS

- Planning
- Organizing
- Problem solving
- Short-term memory
- Movement
- Personality
- Emotions
- Behavior
- Language

Parietal lobe:

- Interprets sensory information, such as taste, temperature, and touch

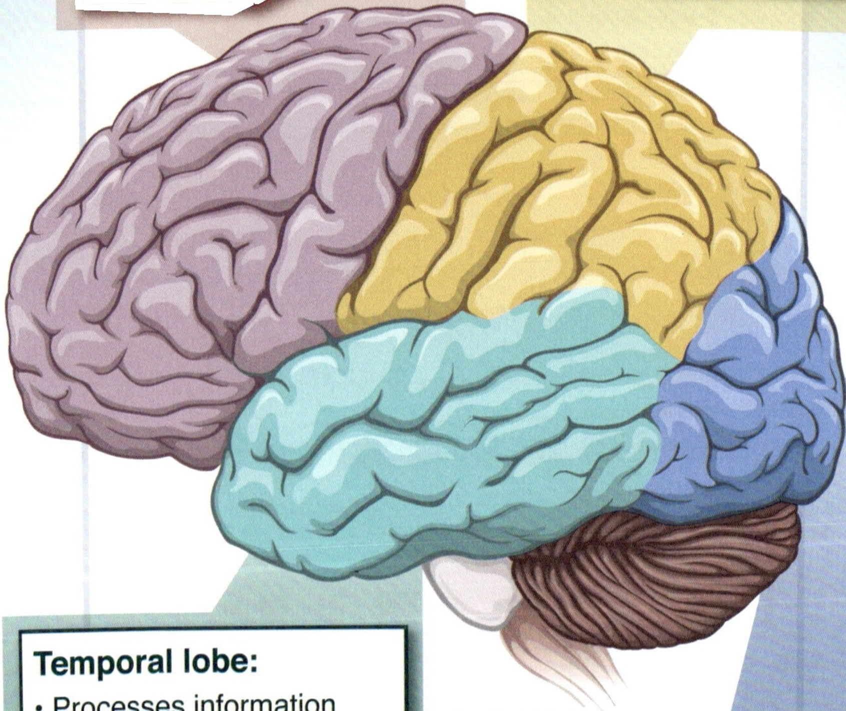

Temporal lobe:

- Processes information from the senses of smell, taste, and sound
- Plays role in memory storage

Occipital lobe:

- Processes images from the eyes
- Links information with images stored in memory

Source: Mayo Foundation for Education and Research, "Slide Show: How Your Brain Works." www.mayoclinic.org.

INTRODUCTION

No One Can Stand Alone

Until recently, psychologists assumed that the only way for human beings to be emotionally healthy and happy was for them to become self-sufficient in their emotional lives. As children mature, the theory went, they go through a process of disengaging from their parents until they no longer need their emotional support. Relationships are nice to have, the experts thought, but independent, psychologically sound adults should not need those relationships to be happy.

It turns out this idea is completely wrong. "When an infant crawls away from her mother, she's not trying to separate from humanity," explains psychiatrist Amy Banks. "Instead, the baby is expanding her relational world; she's moving toward more connections, toward the big world and the people who populate that world."[1] In other words, the process of growing up is not about becoming emotionally self-sufficient; it is about learning how to engage in more complex social relationships.

Human beings need relationships—not only to be happy, but also to be physically and psychologically healthy. Infants are born with a need to connect with adults. In fact, infants' brains and bodies do not develop properly if that connection is absent. Babies who are not touched or soothed in the first months of life are smaller than those who are. They also have weaker immune systems and develop severe emotional disorders that can affect the course of their entire lives. "When emotional deprivation and lack of love occur, physical growth slows down or stops,"[2] explains biologist Inês Varela-Silva. This explains why so many children raised in overseas orphanages are in poor mental and physical health. These places are often so understaffed that caregivers are forced to teach infants how to hold their own bottles because no one is available to feed them. These children go for months or years with little human contact. Many do not survive—not for lack of care, but for lack of love.

Scientists now know that the brain cannot develop normally in isolation. As infants bond with their parents, their brains create millions of connections that link human touch with comfort and security. As they grow, they are able to transfer this emotional connection to others, make friends, and develop a secure and confident sense of self.

Healthy and Unhealthy Identities

Psychologists have also discovered that a healthy personal identity can form only in the midst of healthy relationships. "We have both an internal, embodied identity as 'me' and an interpersonal, interconnected identity as 'we,'" explains psychiatrist Daniel Siegel. "Both *me* and *we* shape our sense of self."[3] In other words, people are inherently predisposed to define themselves through their relationships, a process that starts at birth. Without a foundation of secure, loving relationships, human beings cannot develop a healthy identity.

> **WORDS IN CONTEXT**
>
> **identity**
> A person's self-concept, or how one views oneself. Self-esteem is a core component of identity.

On the other hand, unhealthy or dysfunctional relationships can cause a host of psychological problems—most of them related to identity and a child's ability to relate to others. Children who are rejected by their parents or their peers experience intense shame that affects how they see themselves, which in turn affects all of their future relationships. And adults without friends or long-term romantic partners are more likely to develop physical and mental illnesses. In short, lonely people are less successful, have poorer health, and die younger than those with strong connections to others.

A mother and father play with their young daughter. Parent-child bonding produces changes in the brain that enable children to make friends and develop self-confidence as they grow up.

The Fear of Being Cast Out

When relationships go wrong, people can be cast out or ostracized from their families or peer groups. For decades, scientists have grossly underestimated the effect of social exclusion. It is by far one of the most painful and damaging social experiences for human beings.

Humans are hardwired to live in groups—at one time people depended on their tribe for their very survival. This is why being included in a desirable group is a universally comforting and pleasurable experience for people and why exclusion is so fundamentally painful. Human brain chemistry rewards people for joining together and forging connections by making inclusion feel good and exclusion feel bad.

The pain of social exclusion also explains why young people can so easily be swayed to peer pressure. Teens sometimes do things that they know are wrong, not because they want to rebel or show off—but because it feels so dangerous to go against the group. "Connecting with a peer group can feel like a matter of survival," explains Siegel. "Given the psychological stakes, teens can sacrifice morality for membership."[4] Of course, teens are not the only ones who give in to peer pressure. Psychological studies have confirmed again and again that social pressure can persuade people to do all sorts of terrible things. Most of the German soldiers who slaughtered millions of innocent people during the Holocaust were not monsters or psychopaths. They were normal people who loved their families and friends—and who were persuaded by society that murder was patriotism.

WORDS IN CONTEXT

dysfunctional
Not working as it should. Dysfunctional relationships do not support the emotional well-being of the participants.

The Limits of Psychology

Scientists have a long way to go in gaining a true understanding of the psychology of relationships. New techniques that let researchers see human brains in action have made it obvious that the physical brain and the intangible mind are intertwined in ways scientists are just beginning to understand. These scientists are also learning how much relationships affect brain structure, mental health, and every other aspect of human health, success, and happiness. In fact, in many ways, psychology has become the study of human relationships.

CHAPTER 1

Family Relationships

A human being's very first relationship is by far the most important. Babies are helpless, but they are innately primed to attach to adults—in fact, it is because they are so helpless that they are born seeking comfort and security. Adults are also primed to attach to infants. A baby's cry creates a burst of activity in an adult's brain—a stronger burst, scientists have found, than the reaction to the cry of an animal or other loud, disturbing noise. From the first moments after birth, infants and adults are drawn together by the biology of their brains.

Any loving adult, not only a biological parent, can serve as an infant's primary caretaker. What is important is that the baby is provided with security, attention, touch, and interaction. Without this, babies' brains do not develop normally and will lack the foundation for healthy psychological development.

The First Relationship

During the first several years of life, a child's brain goes through extraordinary changes. The foundations of self—such as personality, language, and ways of relating to others—develop rapidly as new neural pathways and connections are created in the brain. But for this to happen, a child must have a strong bond with his or her primary caregiver. Scientists call the process of forming this first human relationship *attachment*. According to attachment theory, the strength and quality of a child's attachment can affect how he or she forms relationships in later life.

Infants are born with a natural desire to form relationships and attach to adults. Because babies are unable to control their emotions themselves, they rely on their caregivers to give comfort and security. When this comfort is consistent and reliable, a baby becomes securely attached to a caregiver; when it is not, the attachment is said to be insecure. Psychologists can measure attachment by using a test referred to as the "strange situation" scenario, which examines how preschoolers respond to their mothers after a short absence. Those who avoid or look away from their mothers upon their return are insecurely attached; they have learned that their mothers will not soothe them on a reliable basis when they are distressed. However, those who immediately try to reunite with their mothers are securely attached. Securely attached children are better able to confidently explore the world—in part because they know that if they become distressed, they will receive support and comfort.

Forming a secure attachment with a caregiver allows children to form successful relationships later in life. "A good relationship with your parents helps you feel safe enough to approach other people and make a connection with them,"[5] explains psychiatrist Amy Banks. But when that attachment is insecure, people usually have difficulties with relationships in later life and can suffer from depression, anxiety, and a host of other problems related to insecurity and trust issues. They are also more likely to have a hard time creating secure attachments with their own children. This does not necessarily mean that they will be neglectful parents; it simply means that they will have a more difficult time understanding their babies' signals and cues. According to Mary Salter Ainsworth, a psychologist who helped define attachment theory in the 1950s, a sensitive caregiver "picks [the baby] up when he seems to wish it, and puts him down when he wants to explore. . . . On the other hand, the [caregiver] who responds inappropriately tries to socialize with the infant when he is hungry, play with him when he is tired, or feed him when he is trying to initiate social interaction."[6]

Attachment theory is continuing to evolve, and most experts believe that children with insecure attachment can still learn to form healthy, rewarding relationships later in life. And as adults, they can break the cycle and create secure attachments with their own children by learning new parenting skills.

Infants are born with a natural desire to form relationships and attach to adults. Having a secure attachment with a caregiver allows children to form successful relationships with others, such as classmates and teachers.

The Brain Is Wired to Connect

As infants mature, they begin to understand that they are separate beings from their parents. Scientists call this the theory of mind (ToM), or the concept that others have minds that are separate from our own. Before the end of their first year, infants have realized that their parents are not extensions of themselves or forces of nature, but individuals with their own thoughts, preferences, and feelings. And by eighteen months, children are actively trying to figure out what their caregivers are thinking. Scientists believe that this ability to imagine the minds of others evolved in humans as a survival mechanism. "One of the big differences between other animals and us is that we depend on other people for just about everything," explains Alison Gopnik, a professor of philosophy and psychology at the University of California–Berkeley. "And that means that having the ability to imagine other people's minds and thoughts is crucial to being

Theory of Mind and Lying

Recent research has found that the development of ToM gives children the skills they need to tell a lie. A 2015 study published in the journal *Psychological Science* devised a game that encouraged three-year-olds to lie: The children would win a piece of candy only if they lied to an adult about where they had hidden it. The study's authors found that the children who received ToM training were much more likely to lie. As the researchers explain, "Telling a lie successfully requires deliberately creating a false belief in the mind of the lie recipient. . . . [Children with ToM training] were able to consolidate the knowledge and use it adaptively to solve a social problem they were facing."

Of course, very young children are not particularly good liars, and parents can easily tell when their toddlers or preschoolers are not being truthful. This gives parents an opportunity to instill the values of honesty and openness at an early period of child development.

Quoted in "Understanding Others' Thoughts Enables Young Kids to Lie," Association for Psychological Science, October 6, 2015. www.psychologicalscience.org.

a successful human."[7] In essence, without ToM, humans could not have relationships.

Experts like Gopnik believe that the mechanism that allows humans to develop ToM is empathy—the ability to feel, on a physical or emotional level, what others are feeling. Empathy is generated by specialized cells in the brain called mirror neurons. Mirror neurons become active when a person observes another person behaving in a certain way. As these brain cells activate, the observer experiences the same emotions or sensations that they see. This explains why humans often have a strong emotional reaction when they see another person in pain and why behaviors such as laughter or yawning are contagious. According to Banks, "There have been studies that look at emotions in human beings such as disgust, shame, happiness, where the exact same areas of the brain light up in the listener who is reading the feelings of the person talking. We are, literally, hardwired to connect."[8]

Because of the mirror neuron system, infants cry when their parents are angry or upset and feel comforted when their parents are calm and relaxed. As children mature, they can examine their own emotional responses to figure out what their parents are feeling and respond to those feelings. This creates an emotional connection between child and parent, the underpinning of all healthy relationships.

Conflict and Parenting Styles

As children mature and begin to see themselves as individuals who are separate from their parents, the parent-child relationship naturally changes. Children aged two and three become more independent, which can lead to defiance and temper tantrums against parental authority. Older preschool and grade-school children may argue, negotiate, lie, or attempt to manipulate their parents to get what they want. Conflict in the parent-child relationship is normal, and it is an opportunity for parents to teach their children how to manage conflict in other relationships.

> **WORDS IN CONTEXT**
>
> **neurons**
> Nerve cells that transmit electrical or chemical messages throughout the body. There are about 100 billion neurons in the brain alone.

The way in which parents relate to their children and manage these conflicts is called their parenting style. According to most psychologists, the healthiest parenting style is described as *authoritative*. As psychologist Ross Thompson explains:

> Children develop greater competence and self-confidence when parents have high (but reasonable) expectations for children's behavior, communicate well with them, are warm and responsive, and use reasoning (rather than coercion) as preferred responses to children's misbehavior. . . . Authoritative parents are supportive and show interest in their kids' activities but are not overbearing and allow them to make constructive mistakes.[9]

Authoritative parents both model good behavior and clearly explain why bad behavior is not acceptable, which encourages children to accept the parents' values as their own and strengthens the parent-child bond. Psychologists have found that children raised by authoritative parents tend to have better self-esteem and greater self-control.

> **WORDS IN CONTEXT**
>
> **manipulate**
> To control or influence another person in an unfair way, usually without that person's knowledge.

In contrast, *authoritarian* parents also lay down rules of behavior but expect rules to be obeyed simply because they are the parents. As psychologist Diana Baumrind explains, these parents "are obedience- and status-oriented, and expect their orders to be obeyed without explanation."[10] They are less likely to be responsive to their children or acknowledge their children's points of view. Children of authoritarian parents may have more problems with emotional openness with others later in life and tend to have lower self-esteem. The two final parenting styles identified by psychologists are *permissive* and *uninvolved*. Permissive parents are nurturing and responsive, but they tend to make few demands on their children and treat them as peers or friends. Often, children raised by permissive parents have problems with self-discipline, tend to do worse in school, and resist the authority of others. Finally, uninvolved parents make few demands on their children and tend to be unresponsive and uncommunicative. Children of uninvolved parents may suffer from an attachment disorder and develop a negative self-concept. They often lack self-control, have low self-esteem, and have poor relationships later in life.

Sibling Relationships

Another core relationship within families is between siblings. Siblings—especially those who are close in age—can have a huge influence on each other; in fact, by age eleven most siblings have spent about a third of their free time in each other's company. Siblings share the same parents, the same environmental conditions, and the same formative experiences, which can create an extraordinarily strong bond. "There may be no relationship that's closer, finer, harder, sweeter, happier, sadder, more filled with joy or fraught with woe than the relationship we have with our brothers and sisters," says Jeffrey Kluger, author of *The Sibling Effect*. Kluger explains that it is through this bond that children learn how to navigate and manage relationships: "We learn about mentoring, we learn about honesty, caring, confidence. We learn about loyalty, keeping confidence. We learn about conflict avoidance, guilt and compromise, gentleness, caring, empathy, love."[11]

But it is often the conflict in sibling relationships that is the most influential in forming identity. Most siblings fight with each other constantly; in fact, researchers have found that siblings in the two- to four-year-old age group have 6.3 fights per hour. In almost all cases, these fights are about property. Because young children have almost no power, defining what belongs to them is one of the first ways they begin to define themselves, and conflicts with

Siblings that are close in age can have a strong influence on each other. Because they share parents, environment, and many experiences, they can develop extraordinarily close bonds.

Teens, Parents, and Values

Before adolescence, most children have a sense of personal identity that has been strongly influenced by their relationships inside the family unit. But teens are much more influenced by the world outside the family. As they find their place in their social circles and learn about different values people hold, they actively try to figure out who they are. To accomplish this, teens naturally experiment with a variety of identities. For instance, some teens may define themselves as artists or musicians; others may become deeply religious or political; still others may emulate the behavior of a peer group.

Embedded in these identities are values—values that define what a teen believes is just or desirable. Teens who have positive relationships with their parents usually retain at least some of their family's core values. However, when relationships are not positive, it is not uncommon for teens to embrace values that are directly opposed to the values held by their parents. For instance, teens from conservative families may embrace liberal politics, while teens whose parents are atheists may become evangelical Christians. It is also normal for values and identities to shift and change during adolescence as teens explore different ideas and options available to them.

siblings become part of this process. "It's a very important part of the development of personal identity," explains psychologist Catherine Salmon, "the idea that 'What's mine is mine and what's yours is yours.'"[12] Conflicts between siblings also help children practice empathy, negotiation, and compromise. For instance, a 2009 study at Concordia University in Montreal, Canada, found that when parents did not interfere in fights between siblings, siblings were able to practice seeing a situation from another's point of view.

All children naturally seek out their parents' attention and approval. That approval helps shape their identities. For instance, children who are praised for their athletic achievement may define themselves as athletes—especially if this means that their parents will spend extra time coaching them or attending sporting events. However, for siblings, this process is complicated by competition with other children in the family. For this reason, siblings tend to try to win their parents' attention by distinguishing themselves from their brothers or sisters, rather than trying to outdo them in a particular area. Scientists call this process deidentification. For instance, if one sibling is good at sports, the other might avoid sports and instead become a star student, thereby gaining all of a parent's attention and praise in that area. Deidentification explains why siblings tend to have very different identities. "Siblings differentiate from one another in order to fill unique niches within the family and thereby reduce competition and rivalry for family resources," explain researchers Alexander Jensen and Susan McHale. "Over time this process is thought to make siblings increasingly different from one another."[13] In fact, scientists have found that, by the time they reach adulthood, siblings tend to be no more similar to one another than they are to strangers.

Conflict in the Parent-Teen Relationship

Even the strongest parent-child relationships are often marked by increased conflict during the teen years. According to journalist Rachel Cusk, parents of teens often report "stories . . . of slammed doors and verbal abuse, of academic failure, of secrecy and dishonesty."[14] As one of Cusk's friends says about her own teenaged children, "They used to be so sweet. . . . I don't know what happened."[15]

Many of the changes in teenagers' personalities and behaviors are related to the profound changes in the brain and body that occur during puberty. These changes cause teens to be less able to handle stress, which makes them more prone to emotional outbursts. In addition, risk taking becomes more rewarding and exciting, yet the ability to consider the consequences of one's actions is not yet fully developed. "It's not that teens can't reason through the question but they don't have access to split second reasoning in their frontal lobes [of the brain] like adults do," explains neurologist

WORDS IN CONTEXT

frontal lobe

The front part of the brain that lies behind the forehead. The frontal lobe controls advanced mental processes such as thought, reasoning, decision making, and planning.

Frances Jensen. "Their brain's activity isn't conducting fast enough for teens to say to themselves 'Oh, I better not do this.' They go for the risk and afterward realize that they shouldn't have done that."[16]

Emotional outbursts, risk taking, poor judgment, and a teen's desire for more independence usually combine to create conflict in the parent-teen relationship. Parents want to keep their children safe, so it can be difficult to allow them more independence at a time when irresponsible behavior can have dire consequences. Parents worry about drug and alcohol use, automobile accidents, teen pregnancy, and a myriad of other dangers teens face. On the other hand, teenagers want control over their own lives and are frustrated that they are still governed by their parents' rules. Cusk, who is also the parent of a teen, remembers her own teenage years. "As a 13-year-old, I felt both powerless within, and outraged by, the adult world."[17]

When a person enters the teen years, risk-taking often becomes more appealing and rewarding. This, along with other factors, may contribute to conflicts in the relationship between teens and their parents.

Parents who focus on helping teens regulate their behavior while respecting their thoughts and feelings are most successful at helping their children transition into adulthood. According to Thompson, "As children reach adolescence, the parent-child relationship increasingly becomes one of 'coregulation,' in which both the parent(s) and the child recognizes the child's growing competence and autonomy, and together they rebalance authority relations."[18] In other words, successful parents allow their teens to practice regulating their own behavior by giving them more freedom while still monitoring their actions and setting down rules. Psychologists call this behavioral control, and parents who shift to this style of parenting tend to maintain close relationships with their teens and continue to have influence over their values. However, parents who attempt to control their teens psychologically—by criticizing their feelings and ways of thinking—often cause a breakdown of the parent-child relationship. These parents may attempt to manipulate their children's beliefs, feelings, or choices through criticism or shame. Parenting through psychological control can cause a troubled transition to adulthood and lead to psychological difficulties later in life.

When Children Grow Up

When children become adults, they are finally able to view their parents not as the all-powerful gods of their childhood or the hopelessly out-of-touch control freaks of their teen years, but as equals. Parents often shift to the role of advisers, giving their children advice about relationships, marriage, and child rearing. Many parents and children even become close friends. However, other parent-child relationships never move past the teen years—at least on a psychological level. Both parents and their grown children can fall into old patterns of behavior, pushing each other's buttons and rehashing issues that should have been settled long ago.

However, unless there is serious dysfunction, family relationships tend to weather these storms. For adult children, family becomes a touchstone—a link to their past selves and a record of how far they have come. These first relationships become the baseline against which all other relationships are defined. Complex, maddening, good, or bad, family relationships teach us how to connect.

CHAPTER 2

Friendship

According to psychologist Suzanne Degges-White, "Friendships are among the most essential and supportive types of relationships you will ever establish, because while family relationships are (typically) non-negotiable, friendship is a voluntary institution."[19] In other words, friends are the family people choose for themselves. But it turns out they are much more than this. Friends give each other confidence, support, and a sense of belonging. In fact, psychologists now believe that having at least one good friend can be the difference between happiness and misery, health and sickness, or even life and death.

Friendship and Health

Scientists once thought that while friendships are certainly nice to have, they are not necessary for human health and happiness. However, research has revealed that our bodies actually need to connect on an emotional level with others and that having strong friendships is critical to being physically and mentally healthy. "[We] are social animals, and we have evolved to be in groups," explains psychologist Tasha Howe. "We have always needed others for our survival. It's in our genes."[20] Studies have confirmed that people who have strong social connections live longer than those who do not. They also have stronger immune systems and fewer heart problems, are less likely to be depressed or suffer from other mental illnesses, and are better able to tolerate pain.

Scientists believe that friendships improve and protect health because feeling connected to others reduces stress, while feeling isolated increases stress. Although stress hormones like cortisol and adrenaline are important to human survival (they are released to help people face dangerous or life-threatening situations), when these hormones are elevated over long periods of time, they can cause serious mental and physical health problems. In fact, simply feeling lonely or disconnected from others can activate stress hormones, damaging the body over time.

> **WORDS IN CONTEXT**
>
> **hormones**
> Chemicals that control emotion and many major body functions.

It is important to note that it is friendship, not simply the presence of others, that protects against stress. "You can feel terribly isolated when you're around other people,"[21] says psychologist John Cacioppo. This is why a person with one close friend may be healthier—both physically and mentally—than a person with dozens of casual acquaintances. It is the quality of the relationship that is important.

Childhood Friendship and Identity

Making friends requires certain social skills—skills that children begin developing early in life. Toddlers learn sharing and turn taking by playing alongside others under the supervision of an adult. In the preschool years, children begin to gravitate toward other children with similar interests (for instance, an interest in a particular type of toy) and develop friendships that tend to revolve around pretend play. As they make up story lines and choose roles, they practice cooperation, compromise, and mutual support—all crucial skills to developing friendships later in life. At about six years old, children begin to deliberately initiate friendships by sharing their toys and inviting others to play. They also become more adept at resolving conflicts without help from adults. Eventually, they come to believe that friendship is more important than winning an argument or getting their way.

As children progress through elementary school, their relationships—including the feedback they get from their peers—begin to influence their self-concept. A child who can make other children laugh may begin to think of himself as funny, while another child who excels at sports and is cheered by her teammates may think of herself as an athlete. In addition, the likes, dislikes, and opinions of friends become increasingly important. For instance, if a child makes a friend who gets good grades in school, the child may begin to value good grades, try harder in class, and eventually see him- or herself as a good student as well. Of course, children can also take on the negative or undesirable behaviors or values of their friends. Regardless of whether the influence is positive or negative, children frequently adopt the beliefs and behaviors of their friends because it strengthens the friendship and creates a sense of belonging and connection.

As children progress through elementary school, the feedback they receive from their peers starts to influence their self-concept. For example, a child who is cheered by classmates for doing well in a sport may begin to think of himself or herself as an athlete.

Social Rejection

When children have trouble making friends and are excluded from social groups, it can have a devastating effect on their self-esteem and sense of personal identity. Kids who consistently have their bids for friendship rejected often begin to think of themselves as different, bad, or unworthy. Unfortunately, these feelings can cause further isolation. Psychologists have found that loneliness causes the brain to go into self-preservation mode—which means that lonely children try to protect themselves from further rejection and tend to see the actions of others in a negative light. This can cause these children to seem unfriendly or socially awkward to others, which further isolates them. "It's heart-wrenching to see the sadness caused by a child's rejection," explains speech and language pathologist Michelle Winner. "Over time it can build into depression and anxiety."[22]

In the elementary school years, children are frequently excluded because their social skills are not as developed as their peers. For instance, they may have trouble determining if other children are willing to play, or they may be slow to realize that they are being too rough or too bossy. Researchers believe that up to 10 percent of children have a problem understanding nonverbal communication. "Considering that 75 per cent of communication is facial expression and body language, stance, volume and tone of voice—and 25 per cent is language—being sluggish at interpreting these cues can leave them at a serious disadvantage,"[23] explains Winner. Children have difficulties reading social cues for a variety of reasons. Brain-based disorders, poor early socialization, early trauma, and abuse or other problems in the home can all cause a delay in social development.

When children do not learn to create relationships with others, it impacts their future. For instance, a twenty-year study by Pennsylvania State University and Duke University tracked more than seven hundred children and found that those who had limited social skills as kindergarteners were far less likely to earn a college degree. They were also more likely to get arrested, binge drink, and apply for public assistance. According to Kristin Schubert, program director at the Robert Wood Johnson Foundation, which funded the research, "Helping children develop social and emotional skills is one of the most important things we can do to prepare them for a healthy future. . . . From an early age, these skills can determine whether a child goes to college or prison, and whether they end up employed or addicted."[24]

Teen Friendships and Evolution

Teenage friendships can be the most emotionally intense relationships people experience in their lifetime. Unlike younger children, who choose their friends based on shared activities or interests, teens build their friendships on intimacy. Sharing personal thoughts and feelings about themselves, their communities, and the larger world allows teens to process the intense emotions that emerge during adolescence. Having close friends brings comfort, reduces stress, and helps teens feel connected.

> **WORDS IN CONTEXT**
>
> **intimacy**
> An emotionally (and sometimes physically) close and loving connection with another.

The teen years are also a time when children turn away from the relationships with their parents and seek affirmation and comfort elsewhere. According to psychiatrist Daniel Siegel, this is a natural and healthy thing to do. All humans need what Siegel calls the four Ss of attachment: to be seen (or affirmed), to be soothed, to be safe, and to be secure. Children receive these things from their parents, but adults must get them from their peers. Therefore, one of the crucial tasks of an adolescent is to master the ability to form meaningful, lasting relationships.

According to Siegel, teens seek out social relationships with their peers because their brains have been conditioned to do so by millions of years of evolution. "In the wild, if you're a mammal without an adolescent peer group, you are as good as dead," Siegel explains. This is why having friends and fitting in with a social group can feel, to a typical teenager, like a matter of life and death. According to Siegel, "Millions and millions of years of evolution are telling this adolescent, 'If I don't have at least one peer that I'm connected with, I'm going to die.'"[25] Parents often have trouble understanding why teens feel so driven to attend a particular party, to dress in a certain way, or to avoid social embarrassment at all costs. They also wonder how their children, who once shared their values, can suddenly give in to negative peer pressure. The reason, according to Siegel, is that teenagers' brains are telling them that forging social ties and fitting in with their peers is crucial for their very survival.

And in a way, it is. Experts agree that the ability to have close relationships in adulthood is key to physical and mental health, longevity, and overall happiness. And just as poor relationship skills in childhood predict poor outcomes in adulthood, so does having a lack of close friendships in the teen years. For instance, a 2015 study published in *Psychological Science* followed 171 seventh and eighth graders from ages thirteen to twenty-seven.

Teen boys offer support to a distraught friend. Adolescents who consistently seek support from friends at times of stress will continue this behavior into adulthood, strengthening their social connections.

Researchers found that teens who had close friendships and a desire to fit in with their peers had better health in adulthood. Another 2015 study published in the journal *Social Cognitive and Affective Neuroscience* found that teens who had supportive friends were much less likely to engage in risky behaviors that could have a lasting impact on their future, such as shoplifting, riding with a dangerous driver, and having unprotected sex.

Making a Habit of Friendship

One reason that it is so important that teens have close friendships during adolescence is that friendship actually affects the development of the brain. Adolescence is a time when the brain undergoes two significant changes. First, the connections between brain cells, or neurons, that are associated with unused behaviors are gradually pruned away. Second, the connections that are currently used are strengthened and protected. This means that teens who consistently turn to their friends in times of stress are strengthening that behavior pathway. When they are adults, they will automatically reach out to their friends for comfort and support—getting their needs met and further strengthening their social connections.

On the other hand, teens who do not have friends to turn to in times of stress are forced to choose another behavior. This means that their brains will become wired to automatically turn to this behavior when stressed. Unfortunately, many stress-relieving behaviors are destructive. For instance, behaviors like excessive rumination or self-blame can lead to depression or anxiety; alcohol or drug use can lead to addiction; self-soothing with food can lead to obesity, and so forth. Adults with destructive automatic behaviors, or habits, can have a hard time changing them. However, some psychologists and therapists have found that these habits are easier to break once their patients have created a strong social support network.

WORDS IN CONTEXT

habit
A behavior, or series of linked behaviors, that the brain performs automatically.

Mentors: A Special Type of Friendship

A mentor is a person who regularly shares his or her knowledge and experience with a younger or more inexperienced person. Mentors take an active interest in their mentee and can act as a personal adviser, a guide, a friend, and even a champion. Some mentorships are formal, while others develop spontaneously over time. A mentor-mentee relationship is based on trust, respect, and a genuine desire to help and be helped.

Many children develop a special relationship with a favorite teacher or trusted adult—a person they can turn to for advice or guidance when they cannot approach their parents. When this happens, there is often a dramatic improvement in the child's academic performance and self-esteem. "These transformative relationships have protective effects, enhance academic self-efficacy, and promote a sense of purpose and self-worth," explains psychiatrist Valerie Maholmes. Maholmes believes a mentor has the power to give a child hope. The relationships work, she says, "when an adult believes a child can achieve, when someone says 'yes' to a child who asks, 'Do you believe in me?'"

Most people are unsure how to find a mentor. Experts say that the best thing to do is to simply ask a prospective mentor for help, take his or her advice, and then report back. Most people enjoy being asked for help, especially when they can share their knowledge and experience. If all goes well, a mentoring relationship will develop naturally—and both parties will benefit.

Quoted in Jessica Lahey, "The Role of Adult Mentorship in Helping Children Deal with Trauma," *Atlantic*, June 11, 2015. www.theatlantic.com.

Scientists still have a great deal to learn about the brain, and theories about teenage relationships and brain development are constantly evolving. However, it is clear that friendships during the teen years play a key role in adult health and happiness.

Teens, Friends, and Social Media

Teenagers are still developing the mental and emotional skills to navigate complex social relationships. In the past, teens could practice creating and managing friendships on a small stage—details about a fight with a friend, for instance, would circulate only among a small social group. However, with the advent of social media, teen friendships—and the inevitable drama that surrounds them—are often exposed on the Internet for all to see. For teenagers concerned about fitting in and being accepted by their peers, the stakes have never been higher. A single social misstep can be instantly communicated to thousands of people. No wonder teenagers spend so much time on social media, tending to their friendships, curating their online personas, and comparing their social status to the status of others.

The problem is that while social media can help maintain friendships by keeping friends connected to each other, it is a terrible place to forge or strengthen friendships. Instead, social media encourages relationships that are based on shared reputations or social status. Who a person truly is matters much less on social media than who a person appears to be—which is why teens often spend huge amounts of energy creating and maintaining their online personas. Unfortunately, since no one can be truly known via social media alone, deep friendships cannot form. As psychiatrist Saul Levine explains, "Many of these 'cyber-bonds' are often anything but meaningful, and can actually be a way of not engaging deeply with others. In the guise of generating friendships, the Internet can ironically serve to keep people apart. Social media can never replace the authenticity and intimacy of face-to-face interactions."[26] In fact, online connections are more likely to be a source of stress than an antidote to it. Teens still need the comfort and connection provided by face-to-face friendships.

Adult Friendships

Many adults find that they have difficulty making satisfying friendships after they leave high school or college. This is partially because many adults no longer have daily access to a large and varied group of individuals from which to choose their friends. Parents—especially those caring for young children—often are forced to choose their friends from the small circle of other parents in their children's social circle. Some people find friends at work, but this can be difficult if a workplace is isolating or if friendships are discouraged. Most adults quickly learn that finding friends takes effort.

Social media has actually made it easier for adults to find potential friends. Some platforms allow adults to reconnect with childhood friends, while others help people who have similar interests set up social events and gatherings. However, because friendships can easily take a backseat to family and work obligations, finding and maintaining friendships can still be a challenge. However, adults need friends just as much as children and teenagers do, and those without friends are less healthy and less happy than those who have at least one good friend. What is important, explains psychologist Margaret Paul, is to be seen and accepted for who we truly are. "We cannot feel at home with people who do not 'get' us,"[27] she says.

Friendship in Old Age

As adults age, they tend to become more and more isolated. Spouses die or marriages end; children move away; friends retire to faraway cities. According to the US Census Bureau, 46 percent of women and almost a quarter of men over age seventy-five live alone. Loneliness takes its toll—isolated elderly people have higher

The human desire for friendship does not diminish with age. Whether young or old, people need friends to live happy, healthy, fulfilling lives.

blood pressure, more instances of dementia, and a higher mortality rate than older people who feel connected to their friends.

Older people also tend to have a lifetime of experience with social relationships and recognize their value. "They invest more in their remaining connections," says psychiatrist Gary Kennedy. "They optimize friendships, rather than try to maximize them."[28] Some even combat loneliness by moving to assisted living homes—simply because it exposes them to a larger pool of people from which to find friends. For instance, eighty-five-year-old Flo Jakubiak began to feel socially cut off in her home in Arizona. "Nobody there knew I existed,"[29] she

Finding a Tribe

Human beings evolved in extended family groups of about 150 to 300 people called tribes. Members of a tribe are usually linked by common experiences, customs, beliefs, and values. Even though modern civilization has replaced the tribes of yesterday, experts believe that the desire to belong to a tribe is a basic human urge—one that is alive and well today. When people join sports teams, get involved in scouting, start book clubs, or even join online communities, they are following the tribal urge to belong to a group of like-minded people.

However, the word *tribe* has taken on a slightly different meaning in today's society. Psychologists talk about the importance of finding one's tribe or creating a family of choice—a group of unrelated people who affirm and care for each other. "We feel at home with people who support us in our highest good—people who want the very best for us," explains psychologist Margaret Paul. She says that when people find their tribes, they feel visible and accepted. This creates a feeling of safety and belonging—powerful emotions that can inspire deep connections among tribe members that can last a lifetime.

Margaret Paul, "Finding Your Tribe," Huffington Post, June 28, 2014. www.huffingtonpost.com.

told *New York Times* reporter Paula Span. She recognized that her social isolation was making her unhappy, moved to an independent living center, and quickly found friends who shared her interests.

Friendship Is a Lifelong Need

From childhood to old age, people need friendship to live happy, healthy, fulfilling lives. As social worker Barbara Moscowitz explains, "The need we've had our entire lives—people who know us, value us, who bring us joy—that never goes away."[30] To be known and valued, to have company and companionship, to feel as though we matter—these are the things that friendships provide.

CHAPTER 3

Romantic Love

According to psychologist Sara Villanueva, "Romantic love is basically intimacy with the added bonus of sexual attraction and passionate commitment."[31] This is one definition of love, and there are countless others. All attempt to capture in words the heady mixture of passion, admiration, connection, and the deep feeling of being known and validated by another person. The feeling can be so powerful that, according to Villanueva, people are overwhelmed the first time they feel it, making statements such as, "I never knew love could be so . . . amazing, deep, fulfilling, complicated, [and] exhausting."[32] Most people believe that the deep and lasting intimacy that romantic love promises is the ultimate personal relationship, and some think the exciting first stages of love are proof that they have found their soul mate. However, as people gain experience in love and romantic relationships, they begin to understand that creating this intimacy takes a lot of work, patience, understanding, and forgiveness. Still, the rewards of love are worth it. No other type of personal relationship has the ability to bring two people closer together.

A Short History of Love and Marriage

Most people assume that romantic love naturally progresses to marriage or a similar permanent commitment. This, however, is a fairly recent development in human history. Until very recently, people married each other so that they could share their wealth, improve their social status, work together as partners to improve their finances, and of course, raise children. Although people wanted compatible partners, they did not necessarily have to be in love. According to sex therapist Esther Perel, for most of history, having sex outside of one's marriage "was the space for love because love was not a building block nor a foundation nor a motive for being married."[33] For instance, the great romantic poets of the seventeenth and eighteenth centuries did not write sonnets about their wives—they wrote them about their mistresses.

Things are different today—at least in most Western societies. Perel explains, "Love . . . is supposed to be the height of intimacy—you and me against the world." She says that with modern marriage, people are proclaiming to each other, "I'm going to have this communicative experience with you where I'm going to share . . . my internal life, my feelings, my worries, my dreams, my aspirations and you're going to reflect back on me and you're going to validate me. And in our relationship I'm going to transcend my existential aloneness."[34]

> **WORDS IN CONTEXT**
>
> **validated**
> To feel that one's thoughts, feelings, beliefs, or values are understood and accepted by another person.

Of course, most marriages, even those that last, do not live up to this romantic ideal. No one person can fulfill all of another's social and emotional needs, and the stresses of everyday life can cause conflict between even the most devoted partners. Still, married people can and do find deep intimacy with each other, and marriage is still viewed as the ultimate human relationship.

How the Brain Experiences Love

The first stages of romantic love are accompanied by some of the most intense emotions many human beings will ever experience. Love can be both wonderful and terrible. "Love has probably started more schoolyard fights, adult feuds, and outright wars than every other catalyst combined—money, alcohol, drugs, politics, sports, etc.,"[35] explains Robert Weiss, an expert on love and sex addiction.

Experts now know that love provokes such powerful responses because it activates the reward system in the brain—the same

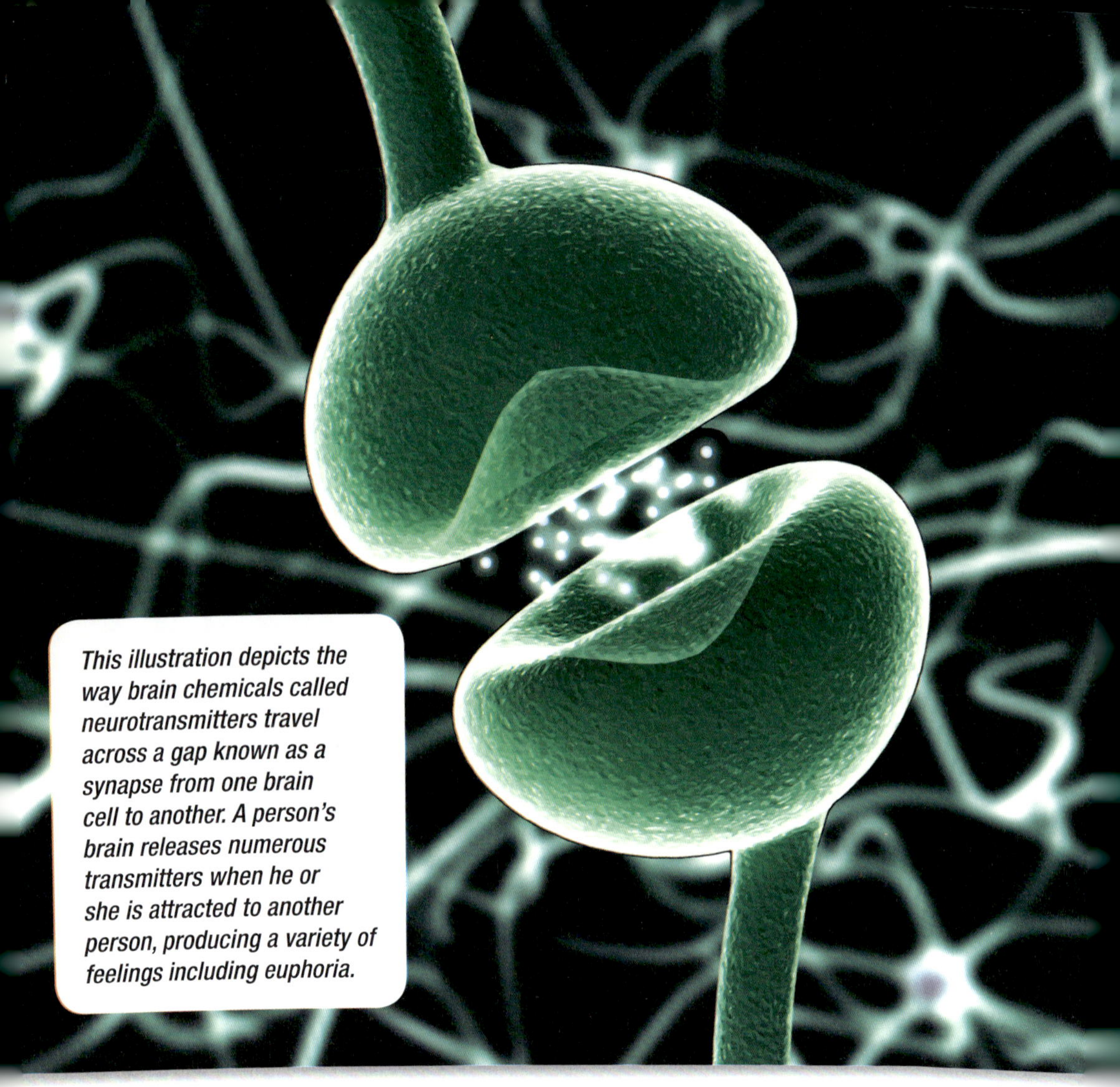

This illustration depicts the way brain chemicals called neurotransmitters travel across a gap known as a synapse from one brain cell to another. A person's brain releases numerous transmitters when he or she is attracted to another person, producing a variety of feelings including euphoria.

reward system that is activated by recreational drugs. According to psychologist JoAnn Deak, "We now know that the chemical changes in parts of the brain when you're in love are equal to that of heroin doses or high cocaine doses."[36] This is why people sometimes go to extreme lengths to be with the one they love—and why it is so painful when love ends. People become, quite literally, addicted to love.

At the first stages of attraction—when people develop what many call a crush or an infatuation—the brain releases a powerful hormone and neurotransmitter called dopamine. Dopamine is associated with pleasure, but it is mostly in charge of making humans pay attention and focus. Dopamine is why people become hyperalert in the presence of a person they would like to date. Other chemicals like adrenaline, epinephrine, and norepinephrine are released as well, causing a rush of excitement and pleasure. This creates a euphoric feeling many describe as "butterflies" in the chest or stomach. When these chemicals combine, humans become infatuated and obsessed with their love interest. As Taryn Hillin, who writes about the science of relationships, explains, "It's our brain's way of saying: *keep going*."[37]

If all goes well and we fall in love, the entire reward system of the brain is activated and flooded with more pleasure-making hormones. These hormones cause people to be euphoric in the presence of their love interest and to crave the other person's company when they are apart. In addition, a section of the brain called the amygdala, which is in charge of judgment, shuts down somewhat—which is why it is so difficult for people to recognize and be wary of the faults in their love interests. Finally, oxytocin, sometimes referred to as the "love hormone," is released during intimacy (it also floods the brain after orgasm). Oxytocin creates the warm, pleasurable feeling of love and connection that causes people to form deep bonds and attachments to one another. Experts agree that our brains are hardwired to have such extreme and pleasurable reactions to romantic love and desire so we will be driven to procreate and raise children as a couple, thus ensuring the survival of the species.

> **WORDS IN CONTEXT**
>
> **reward system**
> A group of structures and connections in the brain that control desire, pleasure, and learning. The reward system influences behavior.

Why We Love Who We Love

Sometimes people fall head over heels with partners who, for whatever reason, cannot provide the emotional intimacy and connection necessary for a committed, fulfilling romantic relationship. This happens in part because the chemicals released in the brain create such powerful feelings that one's better judgment can go out the window. But brain chemistry is not the only reason people are attracted to unsuitable partners. Although scientists are still not entirely sure why people are attracted to one person and not another, there is good evidence that a person's earliest experiences can greatly influence with whom he or she will fall in love.

Many psychologists believe that people seek out relationships that mimic the relationships they had with their parents. Philosopher Alain de Botton, author of *The Course of Love*, explains this idea as follows:

> We believe we are seeking happiness in love, but what we are really after is familiarity. We are looking to re-create, within our adult relationships, the very feelings we knew so well in childhood and which were rarely limited to just tenderness and care. The love most of us will have tasted early on came entwined with other, more destructive dynamics: feelings of wanting to help an adult who was out of control, of being deprived of a parent's warmth or scared of his or her anger, or of not feeling secure enough to communicate our trickier wishes.[38]

According to de Botton, when a person meets someone that evokes the complex love he or she felt for a parent, that other person seems exciting, attractive, and somehow right. For instance, if a woman always loses her temper in traffic, that behavior might remind her boyfriend—on a subconscious level—of the love he has for his short-tempered mother. In fact, he may find that he is usually attracted to women who cannot control their anger and is rarely attracted to those who can. "The fault of the parent remains central to our love choices," de Botton writes. "Without it, we may simply not be able to feel passionate and tender with someone."[39]

Psychological studies have confirmed that people do tend to date and marry partners who are like their opposite-sex parent—regardless of whether they had a good or bad relationship with that parent. And if one partner had an insecure attachment with his or her parents as a child, relationship problems can become

Lesbian, Gay, and Bisexual Relationships Often Start Later

Teens who identify as being lesbian, gay, or bisexual have the same need for love and connection as those who identify as straight. They get crushes and infatuations; they want to date and go steady; they fall in love. However, many cannot simply ask out their crushes and hold hands in the hallway without risking rejection, hostility, or even physical assault from their peers. Because of this, many lesbian, gay, or bisexual individuals do not date until they are adults.

One such person is Jose Reyes, a gay man who did not experience his first kiss until he was twenty-five. When the relationship did not work out, Reyes had an episode of what he calls "Junior High Drama." As he sobbed with disappointment, he realized that he had no experience with heartbreak. "There were other people that I knew that got to experience that in junior high school and I didn't," he says.

People who never get to practice navigating romantic relationships as teens are often shocked by the depth of their emotions the first time they fall in love or experience rejection. "I just want people to know," Reyes says, "it's actually very natural and very normal and okay to have this very dramatic reaction to that experience."

Jose Reyes, "The Impact of Missing Out on 'Junior High Drama,'" YouTube, July 22, 2015. www.youtube.com/watch?v=qP5QZNeOugc.

even worse. People with insecure attachment learned in early childhood that they cannot reliably depend on a parent to make them feel loved and secure. Therefore, when they enter a romantic relationship, they have difficulties giving and receiving love. Some have trouble being intimate or sharing their feelings. Others are constantly anxious about the relationship and insist on commitment too early. In either case these behaviors can be the death knell of a relationship.

Psychologists estimate that about 40 percent of the adult population had an insecure attachment to their primary caregiver when they were children. This may be why romantic relationships often seem so problematic—and why about half of all marriages end in divorce.

Dating and the Teen Years

Until very recently, most young people dated for one reason only: to find a mate and marry. Today people are getting married much later in life. According to the US Census, in 2016 women married for the first time at about age twenty-seven and men at about age twenty-nine—six years later than the average age for both sexes in 1970. Because of this shift, teen dating is no longer about finding a mate and settling down to start a family. As Villanueva

As teens grow older, they move from focusing on the social benefits of being a couple to seeking deeper attachment and connection to their partners. In this way, dating gives teens invaluable experience in learning how to be good relationship partners.

explains, teen dating is now about "an introduction to the world of intimacy, relationship roles, sexual experimentation, and, yes, romantic love. It's almost like practice for the real thing that is yet to come."[40]

> **WORDS IN CONTEXT**
>
> **infatuation**
> The state of experiencing early love and passion. Infatuation is usually intense and short-lived, and it is rarely based on deep connection or attachment.

In the United States teens today start dating at about age thirteen, and by sixteen most have had at least one date. For young teens, the most important part of dating can be its impact on their social status. While some young teens do become emotionally and physically intimate with their partners, most focus on the benefits of being a couple in their social circles. They may hold hands or kiss at school, present themselves as a couple on social media, and socialize as a couple with their friends. By age fifteen or sixteen, romantic relationships become more meaningful and intimate, and by seventeen or eighteen, teens are thinking about their relationships in a more mature way and are seeking deeper attachment and connection with their partners. According to Villanueva, dating throughout the teen years helps adolescents "become healthy, mature, informed individuals who are training to be good relational partners."[41]

Teens, Sex, and Social Media

Unfortunately, the Internet and social media have seriously complicated teen romantic relationships. According to Nancy Jo Sales, author of *American Girls: Social Media and the Secret Lives of Teenagers*, online pornography especially has had a huge influence on how teens relate to each other online. "The porn aesthetic is . . . really engulfing social media," Sales says. "And social media is just full of really explicit sexual content."[42] One result is that teens feel they must create and post sexualized, or "hot," images of themselves online, whether they want to or not. This can cause a host of uncomfortable and confusing feelings. For instance, Sales describes one young girl's reaction to being pressured by a boy to text him a nude picture: "All kinds of thoughts start to go through her head. Like, wow, should I be flattered? Should I be outraged? Should I be insulted? Is this—should I do it? Should I not do it? Well, if I did it, what would it look like? . . . And these are new kinds of things for anybody to have to think about, especially 13-year-old girls."[43]

Many teens see no way to escape the sexualized culture that exists on social media. Sales says that teens are very aware that this environment feels toxic to their emotional well-being. "And yet they can't leave it," she explains. "This is the swamp they're swimming in. This is the world they're enmeshed in, where you have to be on it, or you're not part of the conversation, you're not part of what's happening."[44] In other words, many young teens today feel they have no choice but to confront powerful feelings about sexuality and sexual relationships before they feel ready or equipped to do so.

It is still unclear how the sexualization of social media influences the ways in which teens learn to create and navigate their romantic relationships. However, experts agree that it can be a huge stressor for teens, especially those who do not feel ready to explore love and sex.

Committed Relationships

Experts believe that people who get married (or enter into any long-term, committed relationship) go through a series of adjustments as they learn to share their lives with another individual. In the first stage, which can last a few months to a few years, couples are still in the thrall of the powerful emotions that surround romantic love. But as time progresses and those exciting feelings fade, couples enter a middle stage—a period of adjustment in which they must confront the reality of trying to share a life with another individual. Finances and child rearing are the most common stressors during this time and can cause conflict. Some partners question whether they chose the right mate, while others might withdraw emotionally or physically. However, marriage experts have found that couples who are able to work through the middle stage of marriage often increase their intimacy and connection to each other and settle into what many psychologists refer to as a mature relationship. As anthropologist Helen Fisher explains, this final stage of marriage "is characterized by feelings of calm, security, social comfort, and emotional union."[45]

About 50 percent of married couples are never able to work through the difficulties in the middle stage of marriage and decide to divorce. Divorce is almost always a painful process, even when it is a mutual decision. People struggle with feelings of loss, failure, and guilt, and many must go through a grieving process before they can move on to a new relationship. Like all romantic breakups, divorce hurts.

Married couples who are unable to work through their conflicts may choose to divorce. Even when the decision to divorce is mutual, the process often produces feelings of loss, failure, and guilt.

Why Are Breakups So Painful?

According to neuroscientist Matthew Lieberman, "The term 'love hurts' is not just a metaphor. It's real."[46] Lieberman discovered that physical pain and emotional pain are processed by the brain in the same way. He devised an experiment that scanned people's brains while they were playing a computer game. The game was designed to make the participants feel as though they were being deliberately excluded by other players. The experiment revealed that the parts of the brain that signal alarm and distress during physical pain were activated by the emotional pain of exclusion.

Contempt—the Relationship Killer

John Gottman, a psychologist who studies relationships, wanted to find out if he could predict whether couples would stay together or break up based on how they related to each other. Gottman developed a system that could identify a person's emotions by examining his or her body language and facial expressions moment by moment. He videotaped newlywed couples while they discussed a problem in their relationship, and then he analyzed their facial expressions and body postures to uncover what emotional messages they were sending to each other.

Gottman checked back with the couples over the years to see how their relationships were going and made a remarkable discovery. Ninety-four percent of the couples who displayed contempt toward each other had separated.

Contempt can be identified by brief expressions—a one-sided smirk and crinkling of the eyebrows or a grimace and a rolling of the eyes. According to Ellie Lisitsa, a staff writer for the Gottman Institute, "When we communicate in this state, we are truly mean—treating others with disrespect, mocking them with sarcasm, ridicule, name-calling, mimicking, and/or body language such as eye-rolling. The target of contempt is made to feel despised and worthless." Contempt also makes open, honest communication—the foundation of any long-term partnership—impossible.

Quoted in Zahra Mulroy, "The One Sign Your Relationship Is in Serious Trouble—According to Experts," *Mirror* (London), July 25, 2016. www.mirror.co.uk.

This pain turned out to be so similar to physical pain that other researchers found it could be relieved by over-the-counter pain medication. According to Lieberman, this explains why romantic breakups are so difficult: Social pain is real pain.

Why do human beings experience these feelings? Like physical pain, Lieberman says, emotional pain is a message that something is wrong. The pain of rejection or loss over a broken relationship motivates us to maintain intimate connections to others or to seek them out once more. The brain works to keep us together—by making love feel wonderful and the loss of love feel terrible.

The Most Intimate Relationship

Romantic relationships allow humans to experience a profound level of intimacy. Partners often become deeply attached to one another, which allows them to reexperience the attachment they once felt to their parents. They develop intimate friendships with each other, sharing their thoughts, feelings, dreams and desires. And they enjoy physical and sexual intimacy, which activates brain chemicals responsible for excitement, pleasure, and bonding. Joyful, painful, and endlessly complex, these are the most intimate of human relationships.

CHAPTER 4

When Relationships Go Wrong

Human relationships are never perfect. Parents make mistakes, friends betray each other, romances end in tears, and marriages end in divorce. However painful, these issues fall within the normal range of human experience, and most people who experience them do not suffer any lasting harm.

But relationships can also go terribly wrong. Parents can abuse their children, peers can become tormentors, and marriages can become violent prisons. These severely dysfunctional relationships can affect people long after the trauma has ended, harming their health, their happiness, and their ability to connect again.

Reactive Attachment Disorder

Experts believe that about 40 percent of people have insecure attachments to their parents. Insecure attachment is not a psychological disorder; it simply puts an individual at risk of having some level of difficulty with personal relationships in the future. However, when attachment between a child and a caregiver is severely disrupted—or never occurs in the first place—the consequences are dire. The result can be reactive attachment disorder (RAD), a psychological disorder that can affect all of a child's present and future relationships.

RAD is a relatively new diagnosis in the fifth edition of the *Diagnostic and Statistical Manual of Mental Disorders* (DSM-5)—the official listing of mental health disorders used by health professionals in the United States. According to the DSM-5, children diagnosed with RAD must have experienced extreme neglect that disrupted or prevented early attachment. Children who have a parent with a mental disorder or a serious addiction problem, and children who are placed in a series of low-quality foster homes or other inadequate care facilities at an early age, are most likely to develop RAD.

Children with RAD did not learn to rely on a caregiver for comfort and support in their first months or years of life. Because of this, they react inappropriately when comfort is offered. Some do not seek out comfort when they are upset, and they become irritable, sad, or afraid when hugged or soothed. Others show no fear of unknown adults, are overly affectionate with strangers, and easily follow strange adults into unfamiliar settings. These symptoms show up early in life; to be diagnosed with RAD, a child must show signs of the disorder before age five.

> **WORDS IN CONTEXT**
>
> **neglect**
> In the context of child abuse, a failure to meet a child's basic physical and psychological needs, including the need for love.

RAD is rare among children who are raised by their biological parents. It is more common in children who have been adopted, especially if they did not have a reliable caregiver before the adoption. For instance, Tina Traster did not realize the infant she adopted suffered from an attachment disorder. Julia would not make eye contact, hug Traster back, or cry when she was hurt. By age four, she would run up to strangers and hug them yet be distant, manipulative, and defiant at home. In her book *Rescuing Julia Twice: A Mother's Tale of Russian Adoption and Overcoming Reactive Attachment Disorder*, Traster says that the only way her daughter felt comforted and secure was by controlling her surroundings. "Children like Julia don't feel punished during a time-out—they are relieved," Traster explains. "It [validates] their belief that they are alone in this world."[47]

Research has shown that early deprivation of love and connection causes long-lasting changes in the brain. Because of this, children like Julia have profound difficulties making any healthy human connections and sometimes grow up lacking empathy and displaying antisocial behavior. According to the Institute for Attachment and Child Development, some characteristics associated with RAD in adults include having a lack of remorse, conscience, or compassion for others; lying, stealing, and cheating; and destructive and cruel behavior. All of these characteristics point to a lack of empathy—a necessary component of all healthy human relationships.

Child neglect is a form of abuse. Abused children often come to believe that they are mistreated because they are somehow flawed, leading to deep feelings of shame that can negatively affect their relationships into adulthood.

However, children with RAD can be helped. The deep wounds caused by a lack of attachment can be repaired by loving, attentive caregivers and appropriate therapy. As psychologist Philip Fisher explains, "The brain will recover, if it's allowed to."[48]

Child Abuse

Attachment disorders can sometimes be caused by child abuse. Child abuse is frighteningly prevalent in society; the Centers for Disease Control and Prevention reports that in 2014, over seven hundred thousand children were known to be abused. In fact, experts estimate that one in four children will experience some form of child abuse in their lifetime.

In general, any behavior that causes lasting physical harm to a child or disrupts his or her normal psychological development is considered child abuse. Abuse can be physical, sexual, emotional, or any combination of the three. Neglect is also a form of child abuse.

Child abuse perverts healthy attachment and causes intense feelings of shame in its victims. Shame is an extremely destructive emotion. When people feel guilty, they believe their actions are wrong; when they feel shame, they believe they themselves are somehow flawed. Because children depend on their caregivers for their very lives, they rarely blame them for abuse. Instead, they blame themselves. According to Beverly Engel, author of *It Wasn't Your Fault: Freeing Yourself from the Shame of Childhood Abuse with the Power of Self-Compassion*, "In essence [children who are abused are] saying to themselves, 'My mother is treating me like this because I've been bad,' or, 'I am being neglected because I am unlovable.'"[49]

The shame brought on by childhood abuse affects one's identity, and an identity based on shame can affect every aspect of an adult's life—especially his or her relationships with others. Adults with a shame-based identity often believe if others really knew them, they would be disgusted or reject them. This belief can prevent them from connecting with others or cause them to choose abusive relationships.

Shame can also cause feelings of rage, which Engel says "serves a much-needed self-protective function of both insulating the self against further exposure and actively keeping others away."[50] However, if that rage is never expressed in a healthy way, it can cause adults to lash out against their friends or partners, damaging relationships that would otherwise be healthy and healing. It can also cause adults to abuse their partner or children, and children to bully their siblings and peers. According to the Child Welfare Information Gateway, research suggests that a third of childhood abuse victims will go on to abuse their children. Studies also suggest that about 40 percent of children involved in bullying (those who bully, who are bullied, or who are involved in both) have experienced verbal or physical abuse in the home.

Bullying

Beth, a quiet seventh grader, had always been popular. One day after she had a disagreement with a popular boy, all of her friends decided to eject her from their group. Overnight, Beth's life was turned upside down—no one would speak to her, she had no friends, and she had no idea how to make new ones. Beth was suddenly an outcast.

Millions of children like Beth are bullied every day. Some are physically assaulted; others are regularly humiliated; still others are deliberately isolated by their peers. According to the National Institutes of Health, 54 percent of sixth through tenth graders have been bullied. Though bullying was once thought to be a harmless part of childhood, experts now know that being bullied can have an extremely negative psychological impact. Bullying makes kids much more susceptible to disorders such as anxiety, depression, and addiction—all of which can have deadly outcomes. Violence, school shootings, and suicide have all been linked to bullying.

Researchers such as Ellen Walser deLara have even found that the harmful effects of bullying can persist into adulthood, impacting self-esteem, happiness, and the ability to have meaningful relationships. DeLara interviewed 836 adults for her book, *Bullying Scars: The Impact on Adult Life and Relationships*, and found that three-quarters still suffered emotional problems related

Cyberbullying

According to the website CyberBully Hotline, over 40 percent of teens who are online have been cyberbullied. One in five of these teens say that the bullying has caused them to consider suicide, and one in ten have actually attempted it. These statistics are shocking, as are the many high-profile cases of suicides provoked by online bullies. But since bullying is nothing new, why does cyberbullying—harassing or humiliating someone online, usually via social media—have such a devastating effect?

One reason is that there is very little accountability in an online setting. "When you're not directly in touch with somebody, it's like it puts up a wall," explains psychologist Jennifer Powell-Lunder. "It shuts off your emotion. It's not real and if it's not real, you can do anything." This means that cyberbullying attacks can be much crueler than bullying that happens face-to-face. Another reason is that cyberbullying has a much larger audience. An entire school community can access an embarrassing photograph instantly, for instance, magnifying the humiliation of the victim. And once something is posted online, there is always a chance it will be preserved indefinitely. "This is a new kind of childhood," says Nancy Jo Sales, author of *American Girls: Social Media and the Secret Lives of Teenagers*. "It's a new kind of teenage experience."

Quoted in Rebecca Granet, "Living in Live Time: Social Media and Your Brain," CBS New York, September 19, 2016. http://newyork.cbslocal.com.

to being bullied as children. Her research strongly suggests that bullying can cause lasting psychological damage.

To understand why bullying has such a profoundly negative effect, it is important to view bullying in terms of social relationships. Although there are many different definitions of bullying, at its core it is almost always about singling out and excluding an individual from group membership. Those who are bullied can feel excluded because they are ignored or deliberately isolated, told they are different or not normal, made to feel inferior to—or actively hated by—their peers, or simply too afraid to move freely in a group.

Bullying also tends to occur right at the time when young people are still learning how to make friends and fit into their peer groups. Bullying interrupts this process; instead, children learn that they are different or not worthy—messages that can cause profound and persistent feelings of shame. Although most children can bounce back from occasional rejection, few have enough resilience to withstand prolonged bullying. As Beth recalls, "I wasn't ready for this kind of assault on my self-worth. I couldn't sleep. I felt stuck, I couldn't fix it."[51]

WORDS IN CONTEXT

resilience
The ability to bounce back or recover quickly from psychologically damaging experiences.

Like many kids who are bullied, Beth began to internalize her isolation and shame, which affected her sense of who she was. Once an outgoing and friendly girl, Beth "figured out how to get invisible"[52] to avoid any and all conflict—a pattern that has persisted into adulthood. The betrayal also made it difficult for her to trust people—a key element of any personal relationship. Hundreds of people whom deLara interviewed had the same problem—as adults, some became "people pleasers" like Beth, while others became hostile toward others or asocial. Most were unwilling or unable to trust people enough to establish meaningful relationships. As one interview subject explained, "I feel helpless when it comes to making real friends. . . . I never connect with them due to fear of rejection. Being bullied made me hate people." Another said, "My self-image is messed up. I never really believe that someone likes me. That makes it difficult for me to be in a relationship."[53]

DeLara believes that adults experiencing what she calls adult post-bullying syndrome have had their normal brain development disrupted by the traumatic experience of being bullied. Studies support this idea; for instance, a 2010 study published in the *American Journal of Psychiatry* found that young adults who experienced verbal abuse in childhood—especially in the middle school years—had damage to the corpus callosum, which is the structure that connects the right and left hemispheres of the brain. Damage to the corpus callosum can have a cascading ef-

Research has shown that more than half of sixth through tenth graders have been bullied. Bullying takes many forms, including deliberately excluding someone from a group, but all can have profound and lasting harmful psychological effects.

fect, disrupting normal brain development over time. The result is psychological and behavioral issues, including problems forming healthy relationships.

DeLara's work only confirms what psychologists already know about how crucial it is that people learn how to form healthy relationships during childhood and adolescence. Bullying, as it turns out, is profoundly disruptive to that process.

Domestic Violence

Healthy intimate relationships are built on respect, communication, and compromise. In abusive relationships, however, one partner attempts to control the behavior of the other through intimidation, isolation, psychological manipulation, and physical violence. Abusive behaviors include taking control of a partner's finances, keeping a partner away from friends or family, threatening a partner's reputation, threatening to take custody of the children or harm the family pet, or physically threatening or abusing a partner. According to the US Department of Justice, 1.3 million women and 835,000 men are physically assaulted by an intimate partner each year. The National Coalition Against Domestic Violence reports that one in every four women will be abused by an intimate partner in their lifetime.

Why do abusers have such an intense need for control in their relationships? According to psychiatrist Toby Goldsmith, some abusers have "low self-esteem, extreme jealousy, difficulties in regulating anger and other strong emotions, or . . . feel inferior to the other partner in education and socioeconomic background."[54] Others may have witnessed domestic abuse as children or may have an underlying psychological disorder. However, there is no evidence that any of these factors cause one person to abuse another. In fact, most abusers have the tools to create healthy relationships if they wish—they usually fit in socially at their workplace and are able to maintain friendships. In fact, most intuitively understand enough about relationship psychology to effectively manipulate their victims.

Many experts believe that abusers try to control their partner simply because they believe it is their right. According to New York State's Office for the Prevention of Domestic Violence, abusers have the "belief that abusive behavior is a legitimate way to create and maintain their 'rightful' position of power and privilege within their family—i.e., that they are *entitled* to act as they do."[55] Regardless of what caused this belief, it is the belief itself—not any underlying psychological issue—that is at the root of domestic violence.

Impact of Domestic Violence on Family Relationships

People sometimes question why a victim stays with an abuser. In almost all cases, the victim is simply more afraid of leaving than of staying. Some psychologists claim that an abuser often seeks out

The prolonged stress of being subject to domestic abuse increases victims' risk of suffering major disorders both physical and mental. These mental disorders include depression, anxiety, panic attacks, substance abuse, and sleep disorders such as insomnia.

a certain type of victim—one who is a people pleaser, is afraid of conflict, or experienced abuse as a child. While this is sometimes true, most experts now believe that while victims may be initially attracted to their abuser because of some dysfunctional relationship or experience in their past, they do not stay with their abuser because of this. Victims stay because they believe they have no choice.

The effect of abuse on victims is long-lasting. Victims are much more likely to have mental and physical health problems than the general population, even if they escape their relationships. And because of the effect that prolonged exposure to stress has had on their bodies, they are at higher risk for almost all major diseases and disorders. They are also at higher risk for mental health problems such as depression, anxiety, sleep disorders, panic attacks, and post-traumatic stress disorder. And they are fifteen times more likely to use alcohol and drugs in an attempt to cope with past abuse.

Witnessing domestic violence can also have a profoundly negative effect on children. Children who grow up around violence tend to be more angry and disobedient than other children their age, and they can have a lower level of emotional intelligence than their peers. "Children who are exposed to higher aggression in the household between parents are having more difficulty reading the signals or the signs of others' negative emotions accurately," explains psychologist C. Cybele Raver. "So if they're coming down the stairs at school and another child bumps into them, they may respond in an aggressive way."[56] These children can have problems establishing healthy relationships because they cannot correctly interpret the emotional cues of others.

> **WORDS IN CONTEXT**
>
> **emotional intelligence**
> A person's skill at recognizing, understanding, and managing emotions.

Domestic violence can also have a lasting impact on family bonds between the abuse victim and his or her children. "Abusers typically actively undermine the children's respect for and confidence for the adult victim," explains Liz Roberts, chief program officer at the domestic violence prevention organization Safe Horizon. "They'll say things like, 'It's your mommy's fault that this happened' or 'Your mommy is stupid, that's why she did that.' Or the children will overhear the put downs directed at the adult victim herself." Roberts says that this can have the effect of undermining children's trust that the abused parent can properly care for them. Children can also blame the abused parent for the abuse, which further disrupts family bonds. "There's often a really long journey for families to heal those relationships and to rebuild their trust,"[57] explains Roberts.

Death of a Parent

One of the most painful and life-altering things that can happen to a child is the death of a parent. Children do not fully understand the finality of death until they are about eight years old. Before this age, they have difficulty understanding that their parent will not return. The fact that the parent is absent can cause intense feelings of abandonment, which can lead to anger, guilt, and in some cases the child's belief that he or she is somehow responsible for the death.

Children engage in what psychologists call magical thinking. *Magical thinking* is a term that describes people's tendency to believe that their thoughts or unrelated actions are responsible for an event. For instance, a child who refuses to kiss his or her dying mother may believe that withholding the kiss caused her death. Some psychologists believe that creating this type of explanation is more reassuring to children than the reality of death—which is both terrifying and out of their control. And by taking the blame for the death, a child does not have to be angry at the parent for dying. However, guilt over the death of a parent can cause a pervasive sense of shame that can affect self-esteem. If these feelings of guilt and shame are not resolved, they can lead to developmental and psychological problems in the future.

Abuse Must Not Be Tolerated

Dysfunctional relationships can and do cause lasting emotional and physical damage. When the dysfunction disrupts attachment, children can lose their ability to form healthy relationships, which impacts their future health and happiness. When the dysfunctional relationship is abusive, lives can be destroyed. These relationships are not normal and should not be tolerated by individuals or society. The impact on emotional and physical health is simply too great.

CHAPTER 5

Psychological Disorders and Relationships

Laurel and Catherine had been good friends for over a decade. But when Laurel's depression symptoms flared up, she became convinced that her friend no longer liked her. "When I would call and get her voicemail, depression told me she was screening my calls," Laurel said. "When she was too busy with work to make the two-hour drive to visit me, depression said she would rather do anything than be around me."[58] Eventually, Laurel lashed out at Catherine, seriously damaging their friendship.

Mental illness can have a devastating effect on relationships. According to the National Alliance on Mental Illness, each year about one in five adults experiences some form of mental illness—putting countless relationships under strain. Disorders like depression affect a person's behavior, making him or her more self-involved and less able to see things from another's point of view. This can undercut the love and connection of established relationships and prevent new relationships from forming.

Mental illnesses like depression can cause—or even be caused by—relationship problems, but they are primarily disorders of mood and behavior. However, some mental disorders are defined by their effect on a person's ability to form and maintain relationships. These disorders often have a strong genetic component and are usually present in childhood. Though symptoms can sometimes be treated, there is no cure for these conditions, and some of those afflicted may struggle with their disorder throughout their entire life.

Autism Spectrum Disorder

Autism spectrum disorder (which is usually referred to as autism) is a developmental disability that affects a person's ability to form social relationships. It is a brain-based disorder that begins in early childhood—when children are learning to attach to and connect with adults. Children with autism have difficulties recognizing and interpreting body language, facial expressions, and the complexities of verbal communication, such as tone and inflection. Autism exists on a spectrum from mild to severe. Some people with autism are high functioning (previously, high-functioning autism was known as Asperger's syndrome) and have learned to fit in well with society. Others are described as low functioning and can also suffer from intellectual disability, motor coordination problems, and physical health issues.

Children with autism have trouble grasping the rules of social behavior—such as making eye contact with others—on their own. However, they can learn these rules through intensive intervention, allowing them to be more successful in establishing personal relationships.

> **WORDS IN CONTEXT**
>
> **synaptic connections**
> The connections between neurons that allow information, in the form of chemicals or electrical impulses, to pass from one neuron to another.

Recent research on the brains of people with autism has found evidence that the disorder may be caused by too many synaptic connections. In childhood and adolescence, the brain gradually prunes away the huge number of synaptic connections in a child's growing brain—in part so the brain is not overloaded with too much information. "Impairments that we see in autism seem to be partly due to different parts of the brain talking too much to each other," explains neuroscientist Ralph-Axel Müller. "You need to lose connections in order to develop a fine-tuned system of brain networks, because if all parts of the brain talk to all parts of the brain, all you get is noise."[59]

This means that autistic people are overwhelmed by sensory input. Most people's brains automatically filter all but the most important sights, sounds, smells, and physical sensations that they are exposed to at any given time. For instance, nearly everyone has had the experience of allowing their minds to wander while someone is talking to them—and then realizing they have no idea what was said. However, autistic brains cannot filter out unnecessary information. As Lori Sealy, a writer who has autism, explains, "Everything flows through with equal force. Life is like a continual sensory storm. . . . Everything hits me full on." For Sealy, even the sensory experience of meeting the eyes of another person is extremely difficult. "From my earliest days I can remember my neck shaking and my head drifting down when someone's eyes would 'touch' my own (an eye 'touch' is what it felt like, and it was incredibly uncomfortable—it was moist and squishy and made my skin crawl)."[60]

Some experts believe that this "sensory storm" is what prevents children with autism from learning how to establish personal relationships. As small children overwhelmed by the sights and smells around them, they cannot focus on their caregivers—

which means they do not develop the language and other relational skills most babies do. As they get older, their lack of social skills and focus causes them to have a hard time understanding humor, sarcasm, and other subtleties of human interaction. The rules and conventions of conversation—body language, turn taking, staying on topic—can elude them. Most have trouble correctly identifying emotion in others, and about 50 percent cannot recognize or name their own emotions. It is not that people with autism do not care about others—studies have shown that they feel empathy once they understand another person's emotions. They simply do not know how to connect.

This can be extremely frustrating and painful. As Jasmine O'Neill, a writer who has autism, explains, "Many autistic people affectionately, humorously refer to themselves as aliens. They feel displaced on a vast planet, which has a code of life,

The Gift of Autism

Some people with autism view their condition not as a disorder but simply as a difference—one that gives them a unique perspective on the world and thereby enables them to make remarkable contributions to society. In fact, many people speculate that some of the world's most influential figures, such as Wolfgang Amadeus Mozart and Albert Einstein, were autistic.

Temple Grandin is one such person. Grandin is a professor of animal science who redesigned the way livestock is handled in America. Grandin's autism allowed her to understand the way cows experience their environment, which enabled her to design facilities that greatly reduced the animals' level of fear—and in turn reduced injuries and made livestock farming more humane. "Parents get so worried about the deficits [of children with autism] that they don't build up the strengths, but those skills could turn into a job," said Grandin. Grandin believes the special skills autistic children do have should be nurtured—for their benefit and for society's.

Temple Grandin, "About Temple Grandin," Temple Grandin, PhD, February 11, 2014. www.templegrandin.com.

and understanding they can't ever quite subscribe to."[61] However, with intensive intervention, many people with autism can be taught this code and learn the skills needed to relate to others. As with many developmental disorders of the brain, early diagnosis and intervention are key.

Attention-Deficit/Hyperactivity Disorder

Attention-deficit/hyperactivity disorder (ADHD) is another disorder that appears in early childhood. (If there is no hyperactivity present, the disorder is simply called attention deficit disorder, or ADD.) ADHD is a brain disorder of attention and focus. Focus in the brain is controlled by the hormone dopamine—a feel-good chemical that encourages people to pay attention to the matter at hand. Dopamine also governs both motion and motivation. Children with ADHD do not have as much dopamine circulating in their brain as typical children do. Although they are able to focus on things that they like—children with ADHD may focus for hours on building a model or playing a video game—they have difficulty focusing on things that do not interest them a great deal. This is why children with ADHD often have problems in school—they have a hard time concentrating on work that they find boring or repetitive. In addition, the hyperactivity portion of the disorder can make them impulsive, causing them to say or do things that are inappropriate in a social setting.

Because their behavior is often inappropriate, children with ADHD can experience significant social problems. When playing, they can be aggressive, bossy, and impulsive, which can annoy their peers. They also tend to miss social cues in others, make social mistakes, and have trouble regulating their own emotions. Experts estimate that over 50 percent of children with ADHD have no friends, and those who do have friendships are more likely to have those friendships end unexpectedly—often because they behaved inappropriately.

Peer rejection can have a devastating effect on children with ADHD—in part because their self-esteem may already be low. According to psychologist William Pelham, these children often experience one to two negative social interactions every minute.

Their parents and teachers must constantly correct their behavior, and they face a barrage of negative messages from other people around them. "What that means is that most of these kids' interactions with other people are negative," says Pelham. "They're not the ones invited to birthday parties or over to another kid's house to play."[62] Because of this, many children with ADHD begin to expect rejection and withdrawal from their peers, which puts them even further behind in social development. Their low self-esteem also places them at higher risk of developing depression and anxiety disorders. As they get older, they can be ostracized from social groups or bullied, which further harms their sense of self-worth.

Medication can make a huge difference in these children's lives. ADHD is treated with stimulants such as methylphenidate, also known as Ritalin. Ritalin affects the levels of dopamine in the brain, raising them enough that ADHD sufferers can focus. For

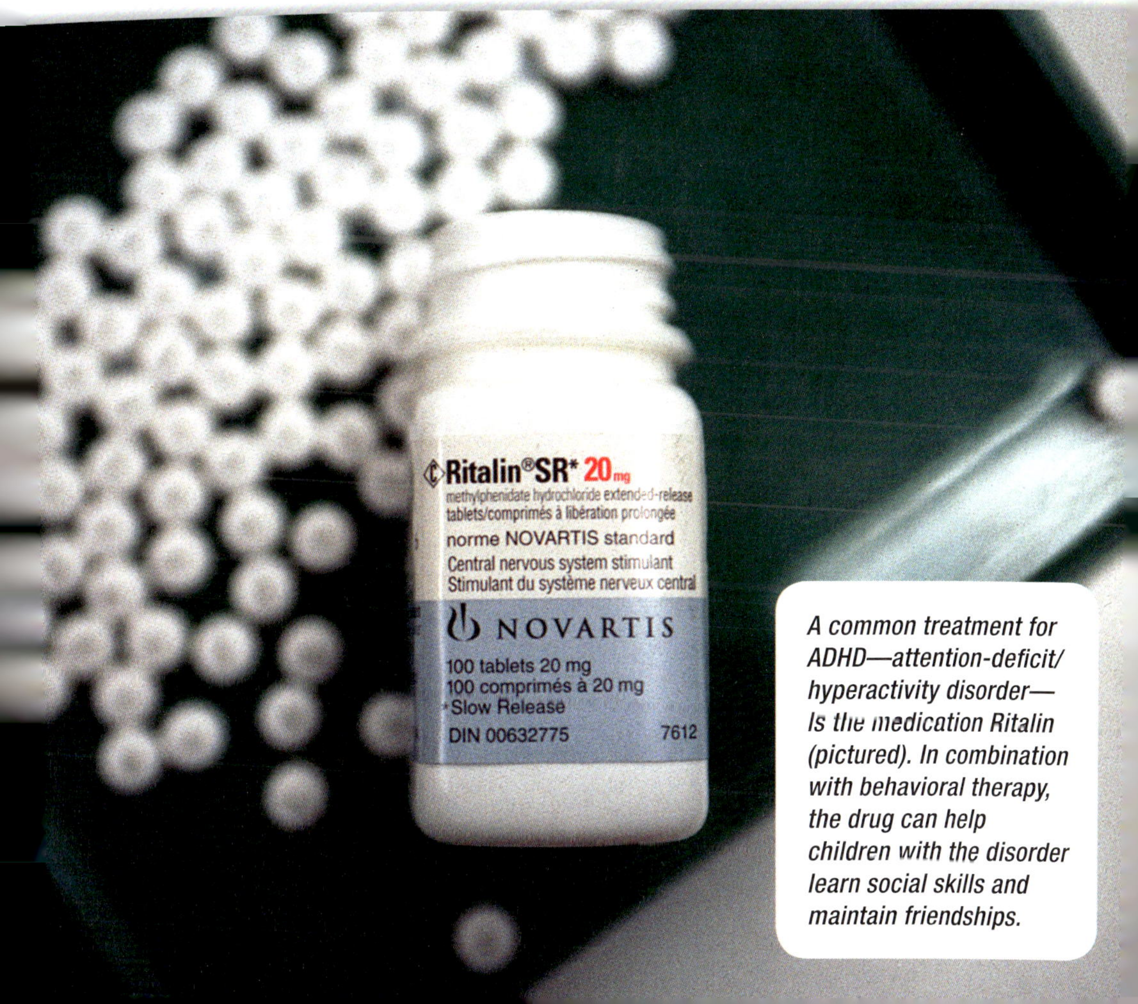

A common treatment for ADHD—attention-deficit/hyperactivity disorder—Is the medication Ritalin (pictured). In combination with behavioral therapy, the drug can help children with the disorder learn social skills and maintain friendships.

Ethan, an eight-year-old boy with ADHD, medication allows him to relate better to others. "It doesn't really feel different," he says about his medication. "It just changes the way other people feel about me."[63]

However, medication without behavioral therapy cannot help children learn social skills and maintain friendships. For that, experts say that parents must get involved, supervising play dates and working with their children at home under the guidance of a behavioral therapist. According to Pelham, parenting and behavior therapy is "a much longer term process, but it's what lays down new neuronal skills based on learning which is much different than taking a pill that lets in a flood of dopamine and changes the child's brain for a moment."[64] In fact, some studies show that

Dr. James Fallon, Psychopath

James Fallon, a noted neuroscientist who studies psychopathy, discovered during his research that he himself is a psychopath. Fallon was reviewing brain scans of imprisoned psychopaths when he noticed something strange—one of the "normal" scans in the control group looked exactly like a psychopathic brain. Thinking there must be a mistake, Fallon checked to see who the scan belonged to. To his dismay, it was his own.

Even though he maintains good relationships with his family and friends, Fallon says that he does not feel an emotional connection to them. He also admits that he constantly manipulates others so that they see him the way he wishes to be seen. "Sometimes I'll make up things so it appears I was wrong," he explains. "It makes me more approachable, more believable. . . . I seem like a nice guy, but I want to be clear—I'm not as nice as I seem to be."

Once Fallon realized he was a psychopath, he started making an effort to be more honest in his relationships. "I'm actually trying to catch myself from trying to manipulate people all the time," he explains. He sees the process as a game. "I'm my own best opponent. If I can beat myself, I've won."

Quoted in Roc Morin, "Dr. James Fallon Makes Being a Psychopath Look like Fun," *Vice*, October 5, 2014. www.vice.com.

almost 40 percent of children who start behavior therapy never need medication.

Some experts believe that ADHD is not really a disorder but an adaptation—a type of brain chemistry that evolved for a specific purpose. Before agriculture was invented about ten thousand years ago, human beings were hunter-gatherers. "As hunters," writes psychiatrist Richard Friedman, "we had to adapt to an ever-changing environment where the dangers were as unpredictable as our next meal. In such a context, having a rapidly shifting but intense attention span and a taste for novelty would have proved highly advantageous."[65] In other words, people with ADHD may have been extremely successful had they lived in a different time.

Personality Disorders

Personality disorders are not well understood by mental health professionals. Currently, psychologists have identified ten different personality disorders, but these designations have changed over time. Many psychiatrists believe that personality disorders are not illnesses but are extreme expressions of personality traits that are maladaptive and cause problems with human relationships.

> **WORDS IN CONTEXT**
>
> **maladaptive**
> When a behavior or way of thinking is not helpful or positive.

A person's personality is made up of hundreds of traits. When taken together, these traits shape a person's identity. For example, a person who is extroverted (personality trait) may see herself as the life of the party (identity), while a person who likes to listen (personality trait) may see himself as compassionate (identity). Personality traits also tend to be adaptable—for instance, shy people may become the life of the party when they are celebrating with their closest friends.

However, people with personality disorders have rigid and extreme personality traits that interfere with their relationships. They also rarely recognize that they themselves are the problem. For instance, people with paranoid personality disorder honestly believe that others are against them; therefore, they think that the problems in their lives are the fault of others. People with narcissistic personality disorder really do think that they are more important than others; therefore, they believe they have the right to expect everyone to hold them in high regard—and a right to be angry when others do not. And people with an antisocial personality—characterized by aggressiveness, lack of empathy, and hostility toward authority—blame everyone but themselves when they end up in jail. For this reason, people with personality disorders rarely seek help from mental health professionals.

Borderline Personality Disorder

There is one type of personality disorder that mental health professionals commonly see in their practice: borderline personality disorder. Borderlines, as they are commonly called, have a poorly formed sense of self and an intense fear of abandonment. Their emotions often become so heightened that their thinking can become paranoid and delusional. And even though they have an intense need to be with others, their impulsive and manipulative behavior often causes them to sabotage relationships.

> **WORDS IN CONTEXT**
>
> **delusional**
> Believing things that cannot be true.

For these reasons, borderlines tend to experience a great deal of emotional pain and suffering. Many also suffer from other disorders; they are more likely to abuse substances, develop eating disorders, and deliberately harm themselves. In addition, up to 70 percent have one or more mood disorders, such as depression.

Borderlines often seek out mental health professionals for help with one of these conditions, unaware that their maladaptive personalities are at the root of their problems. In addition, up to 50 percent have features of narcissistic and/or antisocial personality disorder—both of which are characterized by arrogance and a disregard for others. This cocktail of conflicting personality traits—an unstable self-image paired with an inflated sense of importance, fear of abandonment paired with a disregard for the feelings of others—makes most borderlines extremely difficult to treat.

Borderlines also tend to be master manipulators in relationships, and they often create chaotic situations in a misguided attempt to protect themselves or avoid abandonment. Psychologist George Simon describes the behavior of one of his borderline patients:

> He would latch onto relationship partners with such intensity that he gave them little breathing room. But equally fearful of both eventual maltreatment as well as emotional "abandonment," he would engage in a wide variety of behaviors (e.g., dramatic self-harm threats and gestures, displays of intense raw emotion, hateful, venom-spewed rants followed by . . . sobbing, clingy behavior and begging not to leave, etc.) that would rightfully "test" the level of commitment of any relationship partner.[66]

Emotional blackmail is rarely effective in long-term relationships. This means that a borderline's fear of abandonment often comes true, creating a self-perpetuating cycle. For this reason, many borderlines are never able to establish healthy long-term relationships.

Psychopathy

Fictional psychopaths including Hannibal Lecter, Dexter, and the Joker have been glamorized by pop culture, but few real psychopaths are actually as brilliant and charming as these characters. Even fewer are violent serial killers (though many experts believe that nearly all serial killers are psychopaths). Yet psychopaths are markedly different from the rest of humanity. And many are very dangerous.

People with psychopathy (also known as sociopathy) do not experience the emotions involved in human relationships. They do not feel the joy of connection or the sting of rejection. They cannot feel love or shame. Most understand these feelings on an intellectual level, and many seem charming and trustworthy

A group of friends poses for a photograph. Human brains are hardwired to seek emotional connection with others as a main source of fulfillment.

because they have become very good at mimicking emotional responses. But they cannot feel empathy or the rewards of human connection.

Most psychopaths view others merely as tools to get what they want. What they want varies, but many experts believe the primary motivation of the psychopath is power. Power can take many forms—some psychopaths delight in starting gossip or ruining reputations; others enjoy sexual conquests; still others may strive to become wealthy or influential at any cost. Those who are sadistic may harm others. Teens with psychopathic tendencies (children cannot be diagnosed with psychopathy) might be bullies, or they might be at the top of the social ladder, using their ability to mimic emotions to charm their peers and convince them to do what they want.

Psychopaths have less electrical activity than others in the orbital cortex, a region of the brain associated with empathy and moral behavior. Scientists know this because when they show psychopaths disturbing pictures—of people and animals being harmed, for instance—their orbital cortexes do not activate. While these brain scans are useful in spotting a psychopath, they are not conclusive, and psychopathy can be diagnosed only through an extensive interview by a trained professional. Even then, diagnosis can still be difficult—psychopaths are often good at convincing others that they are harmless or misunderstood.

There is no cure for psychopathy, which affects about 1 percent of the population. Some experts believe it is not a disorder at all but an adaptive variation. According to psychologist Robert Hare, one of the world's foremost experts on psychopathy, "From an evolutionary perspective . . . they're properly designed for engagement in predatory behaviors. . . . A psychopath I met in my research once told me that using his head instead of his heart gave him an advantage. He saw himself as 'a cat in a world of mice.'"[67]

WORDS IN CONTEXT

sadistic
Getting pleasure from the mental or physical pain of others.

Love Disrupted

Psychological disorders that prevent the formation of healthy relationships disrupt and pervert the main source of fulfillment for human beings—emotional connection with others. Regardless of whether these disorders are true mental illnesses or normal—but extreme—variations on the makeup of the human brain, the result is the same: They prevent those who suffer from them from experiencing love. A capacity for love—of family members, friends, and romantic partners—shapes the brain and defines what it is to be human. Humans are, quite simply, hardwired to connect.

SOURCE NOTES

Introduction: No One Can Stand Alone

1. Amy Banks, *Wired to Connect: The Surprising Link Between Brain Science and Strong, Healthy Relationships*. New York: Penguin, 2015. Kindle edition.
2. Inês Varela-Silva, "Can a Lack of Love Be Deadly?," Conversation, May 19, 2016. http://theconversation.com.
3. Daniel Siegel, "How the Teen Brain Transforms Relationships," Greater Good, August 12, 2014. http://greatergood.berkeley.edu.
4. Siegel, "How the Teen Brain Transforms Relationships."

Chapter 1: Family Relationships

5. Banks, *Wired to Connect*.
6. Quoted in Bethany Saltman, "Can Attachment Theory Explain Our Relationships?," *New York Magazine*, June 2016. http://nymag.com.
7. Quoted in Rose Lichter-Marck, "Why Can't I Be You: Alison Gopnik," *Rookie*, July 25, 2014. www.rookiemag.com.
8. Quoted in Rebecca Eanes, "Wired to Connect: Discipline Shouldn't Hurt," *Parenting Beyond Punishment* (blog), June 7, 2016. http://parentingbeyondpunishment.com.
9. Ross Thompson, "Social and Personality Development in Childhood," Noba, 2016. http://nobaproject.com.
10. Quoted in Kendra Cherry, "Parenting Styles: What They Are and Why They Matter," Verywell, September 5, 2016. www.verywell.com.
11. Quoted in Guy Raz, "What Makes Siblings Bond?," *TED Radio Hour*, NPR, April 25, 2014. www.npr.org.
12. Quoted in Jeffrey Kluger, "Siblings: How They Shape Each Other . . . and How Parents Can Help," *Time*, September 16, 2015. http://time.com.
13. Alexander Jensen and Susan McHale, "What Makes Siblings Different? The Development of Sibling Differences in Academ-

ic Achievement and Interests," *Journal of Family Psychology*, June 29, 2015. www.ncbi.nlm.nih.gov.
14. Rachel Cusk, "Raising Teenagers: The Mother of All Problems," *New York Times*, March 19, 2015. www.nytimes.com.
15. Quoted in Cusk, "Raising Teenagers."
16. Quoted in Grown & Flown, "The Teenage Brain: What Parents Need to Know," March 12, 2015. http://grownandflown.com.
17. Cusk, "Raising Teenagers."
18. Thompson, "Social and Personality Development in Childhood."

Chapter 2: Friendship

19. Suzanne Degges-White, "10 Enduring Truths About Friendship," *Lifetime Connections* (blog), *Psychology Today*, August 10, 2016. www.psychologytoday.com.
20. Quoted in Tom Valeo, "Good Friends Are Good for You," WebMD, October 7, 2016. www.webmd.com.
21. Quoted in Anna Miller, "Friends Wanted," *Monitor on Psychology*, January 2014. www.apa.org.
22. Quoted in Tanith Carey, "Does Your Child Struggle to Make Friends? They Could Be Suffering from Social Dyslexia," *Telegraph* (London), August 31, 2016. www.telegraph.co.uk.
23. Quoted in Carey, "Does Your Child Struggle to Make Friends?"
24. Quoted in Drake Baer and Rachel Gillett, "Science Says Parents of Successful Kids Have These 9 Things in Common," Business Insider, July 29, 2015. www.msn.com.
25. Daniel Siegel, "Why Teens Turn from Parents to Peers," video, Greater Good, July 2014. http://greatergood.berkeley.edu.
26. Saul Levine, "The Importance of Friendship," *Our Emotional Footprint* (blog), *Psychology Today*, February 1, 2016. www.psychologytoday.com.
27. Margaret Paul, "Finding Your Tribe," *Huffington Post*, June 28, 2014. www.huffingtonpost.com.
28. Quoted in Paula Span, "Loneliness Can Be Deadly for Elders; Friends Are the Antidote," *New York Times*, December 30, 2016. www.nytimes.com.

29. Quoted in Span, "Loneliness Can Be Deadly for Elders; Friends Are the Antidote."
30. Quoted in Span, "Loneliness Can Be Deadly for Elders; Friends Are the Antidote."

Chapter 3: Romantic Love

31. Sara Villanueva, "Teen Love & Dating in Today's New World," *How to Parent a Teen* (blog), *Psychology Today*, December 22, 2015. www.psychologytoday.com.
32. Villanueva, "Teen Love & Dating in Today's New World."
33. Esther Perel, "Esther Perel on the Nature of Erotic Desire," transcript, Big Think, September 11, 2014. http://bigthink.com.
34. Perel, "Esther Perel on the Nature of Erotic Desire."
35. Robert Weiss, "This Is Your Brain on Love," *Love and Sex in the Digital Age* (blog), *Psychology Today*, January 28, 2015. www.psychologytoday.com.
36. Quoted in Kelly Dickerson, "Love's Effect on the Brain Is as Powerful as Heroin or Cocaine," Business Insider, October 12, 2015. www.businessinsider.com.
37. Taryn Hillin, "In Your Head: This Is Your Brain on Love," Fusion, February 13, 2015. http://fusion.net.
38. Quoted in Maria Popova, "Why Our Partners Drive Us Mad: Philosopher Alain de Botton to the Central Foible of the Human Heart and How to Heal It," *Brain Pickings* (blog), December 9, 2016. www.brainpickings.org.
39. Quoted in Popova, "Why Our Partners Drive Us Mad."
40. Villanueva, "Teen Love & Dating in Today's New World."
41. Villanueva, "Teen Love & Dating in Today's New World."
42. Quoted in Hari Sreenivasan, "Sex, Social Media and the Pressure on Teenage Girls," *PBS NewsHour*, April 4, 2016. www.pbs.org.
43. Quoted in Sreenivasan, "Sex, Social Media and the Pressure on Teenage Girls."
44. Quoted in Sreenivasan, "Sex, Social Media and the Pressure on Teenage Girls."
45. Quoted in Amanda Chatel, "How Love Changes over Time: From Lust to Attachment, Chemically Speaking," Bustle, August 21, 2014. www.bustle.com.

46. Quoted in Ruth Ostrow, "Neuroscientist Matthew Lieberman Says Love Really Does Hurt," *Australian* (Surry Hills, New South Wales), July 17, 2015. http://at.theaustralian.com.au.

Chapter 4: When Relationships Go Wrong

47. Tina Traster, "The Elusive, Manipulative Adopted Child," *Atlantic*, June 10, 2014. www.theatlantic.com.
48. Quoted in Kirsten Weir, "The Lasting Impact of Neglect," *Monitor on Psychology*, June 2014. www.apa.org.
49. Beverly Engel, "Healing the Shame of Childhood Abuse Through Self-Compassion," *The Compassion Chronicles* (blog), *Psychology Today*, January 15, 2015. www.psychologytoday.com.
50. Engel, "Healing the Shame of Childhood Abuse Through Self-Compassion."
51. Quoted in Ellen Walser deLara, *Bullying Scars: The Impact on Adult Life and Relationships*. New York: Oxford University Press, 2016. Kindle edition.
52. Quoted in DeLara, *Bullying Scars*.
53. Quoted in DeLara, *Bullying Scars*.
54. Toby Goldsmith, "What Causes Domestic Violence?," Psych Central, July 17, 2016. http://psychcentral.com.
55. New York State Office for the Prevention of Domestic Violence, "Understanding Domestic Abusers," December 28, 2016. www.opdv.ny.gov.
56. Quoted in Tara Culp-Ressler, "The Hidden Consequences of Domestic Violence Lingers for Decades," *ThinkProgress* (blog), September 26, 2014. https://thinkprogress.org.
57. Quoted in Culp-Ressler, "The Hidden Consequences of Domestic Violence Lingers for Decades."

Chapter 5: Psychological Disorders and Relationships

58. Quoted in Jenny Kutner, "What Nobody Ever Tells You About How Depression Affects Your Adult Friendships," Mic, September 23, 2015. https://mic.com.
59. Quoted in Pam Belluck, "Study Finds That Brains with Autism Fail to Trim Synapses as They Develop," *New York Times*, August 21, 2014. www.nytimes.com.

60. Lori Sealy, "My Answer to the Question 'What Does Autism Feel Like?,'" Mighty, April 21, 2016. https://themighty.com.
61. Quoted in Christopher Badcock, "The Aliens Have Landed!," *The Imprinted Brain* (blog), *Psychology Today*, December 16, 2015. www.psychologytoday.com.
62. Quoted in Denise Foley, "Growing Up with ADHD," *Time,* November 7, 2014. http://time.com.
63. Ethan, "How Does It Feel to Have ADHD: A Kid's Perspective," Viralist, December 6, 2016. http://sjbuzz.net.
64. Quoted in Foley, "Growing Up with ADHD."
65. Richard Friedman, "A Natural Fix for ADHD," *New York Times*, October 31, 2014. www.nytimes.com.
66. George Simon, "Borderline Personalities in Relationships," Dr. George Simon, September 19, 2014. www.manipulative-people.com.
67. Quoted in Danielle Egan, "Into the Mind of a Psychopath," *Discover*, May 4, 2016. http://discovermagazine.com.

For Further Research

Books

Amy Banks, *Wired to Connect: The Surprising Link Between Brain Science and Strong, Healthy Relationships*. New York: Penguin, 2015.

Ellen Walser deLara, *Bullying Scars: The Impact on Adult Life and Relationships*. New York: Oxford University Press, 2016.

James Fallon, *The Psychopath Inside*. New York: Penguin, 2014.

Temple Grandin, *The Way I See It: A Personal Look at Autism and Asperger's*. Arlington, TX: Future Horizons, 2015.

Terry Levy and Michael Orlans, *Attachment, Trauma and Healing*. 2nd ed. London: Kingsley, 2014.

Nancy Jo Sales, *American Girls: Social Media and the Secret Lives of Teenagers*. New York: Penguin, 2016.

Daniel Siegel, *Brainstorm: The Power and Purpose of the Teenage Brain*. New York: Penguin, 2016.

Internet Sources

Rachel Cusk, "Raising Teenagers: The Mother of All Problems," *New York Times*, March 19, 2015. www.nytimes.com/2015/03/22/magazine/raising-teenagers-the-mother-of-all-problems.html?_r=0.

Danielle Egan, "Into the Mind of a Psychopath," *Discover*, May 4, 2016. http://discovermagazine.com/2016/june/12-psychopath-and-the-hare.

Taryn Hillin, "In Your Head: This Is Your Brain on Love," Fusion, February 13, 2015. http://fusion.net/story/48571/your-brain-on-love-oxytocin-dopamine.

Jeffrey Kluger, "Siblings: How They Shape Each Other . . . and How Parents Can Help," *Time*, September 16, 2015. http://time.com/siblings-how-parents-can-help-them-get-along.

Bethany Saltman, "Can Attachment Theory Explain Our Relationships?," *New York Magazine*, June 2016. http://nymag.com/thecut/2016/06/attachment-theory-motherhood-c-v-r.html.

Ross Thompson, "Social and Personality Development in Childhood," Noba, 2016. http://nobaproject.com/modules/social-and-personality-development-in-childhood.

Websites

Anatomy of Love (https://theanatomyoflove.com). Neuroscientist Lucy Brown and biological anthropologist Helen Fisher have joined forces to look at love from a neuropsychological perspective. The educational site features articles, videos, and relationship quizzes.

Science of Relationships (www.scienceofrelationships.com). Science of Relationships is devoted to unbiased, accurate, and accessible science writing about relationships. The website contains hundreds of articles written by psychologists and other mental health professionals.

INDEX

Note: Boldface page numbers indicate illustrations.

PICTURE CREDITS

Cover: iStockphoto.com/Digital Skillet

4: Maury Aaseng

7: monkeybusinessimages/iStock.com

11: FatCamera/iStock.com

15: Aldo Murillo/iStock.com

18: emyerson/iStock.com

22: FatCamera/iStock.com

25: diego_cervo/iStock.com

29: monkeybusinessimages/iStock.com

34: Depositphotos.com

38: KapturePhotoSolutions/iStock.com

41: AntonioGuillem/iStock.com

46: miroslavmisiura/iStock.com

51: Petrenko Andriy/Shutterstock

53: KatarzynaBialasiewicz/iStock.com

57: Lordin/iStock.com

61: Vince Talotta/Toronto Star/ZUMAPRESS/Newscom

66: apomares/iStock.com

ABOUT THE AUTHOR

Christine Wilcox writes fiction and nonfiction for young adults and adults. She has worked as an editor, an instructional designer, and a writing instructor. She lives in Richmond, Virginia, with her husband, David, and her son, Doug.